Discover Mayflower
Journey to the New World

written and illustrated by Phil Sheppard

About this book

This book was created in partnership with Doncaster Council to commemorate 400 years since the Pilgrims arrived in America.

About the author

Phil Sheppard is an author and illustrator from Doncaster, South Yorkshire. His books include 'Lollipopman: Superhero of the Highway', 'Sheep Ahoy!' and 'Discover Doncaster!'. Find out more by visiting www.philshepp.com.

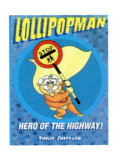

Teaching resources

Teachers can download reading comprehensions, lesson plans and other resources connected with this book by visiting www.tes.com and searching for 'Doncaster Mayflower 400'.

Contents

Cape Cod!

King James

sleeves & collars

Hello, we're the Mayflower mice!

Join us on a voyage to unknown lands in search of adventure, discovery...

...and new kinds of CHEESE!

Our story starts in Scrooby near Doncaster in 1606 when a group of people called the Separatists moved in.

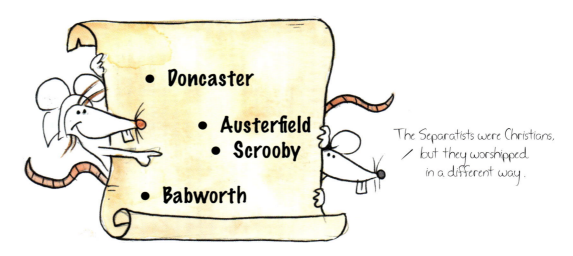

- **Doncaster**
- **Austerfield**
- **Scrooby**
- **Babworth**

The Separatists were Christians, but they worshipped in a different way.

Shhh! Can you imagine having to live in secret?
That's what the Separatists had to do when they were in Doncaster... only us mice knew they were there.
They hid in a posting station (that's where people changed their horses and carriages) and tried to worship in secret.

Why were these people so important?
Because they were brave... they were determined... they were clever!
Later they would become **Pilgrims** and set up home in a place called... AMERICA!

1

Meet the Pilgrims

William Brewster was in charge. He was an older member of the group and very well respected.

William Butten was a young boy. When his father died, his mother was too poor to support him so he became a servant to the Mayflower's doctor.

Mary Brewster - that was William's wife and mother to their six children. Mary was an incredibly brave woman, travelling half way round the world to start a new and exciting life!

John Carver from Doncaster was a natural leader. He became the first governor when the Pilgrims reached America.

William Bradford was a teenager when he went to school in Doncaster. He would have had to walk 8 miles to get there from his home in Auster-field! He was also dedicated to a church in Babworth... that's 8 miles in the other direction! I bet he had sore feet!

Susanna White was mother of a son called Resolved. She was married to another William... William White.

Why were so many people called William?

Where there's a Will, there's... another Will!

Escape from tyranny

So why did the Pilgrims need to hide?

One answer... KING JAMES!

That's him!

booo!

King James' law said that people could only **worship** in HIS churches. But would the Pilgrims obey these religious rules? Of course not! This made King James angry. And when King James got angry, he sent his soldiers to...

- spy on the Pilgrims
- forcefully break up their meetings
- drag them from their homes
- kidnap their children
- put Pilgrims in jail

He was more rotten than this cheese!

Did you know...
King James was the one
Guy Fawkes tried to blow up!

TO KING JAMES

To the Pilgrims, their religion was everything. It meant more to them than their money, their home, even their country. So, eventually they decided...

ENOUGH IS ENOUGH! WE'RE OFF!

Ah-ah-ahhhh!

Excrement? That's poo! Yuck!

They wanted to go to Holland - but people couldn't just leave the country, that annoyed tetchy old King James. So they had to sneak off, a few at a time.

HOLLAND OR BUST!

Escape to Holland

The Pilgrims were happy in Holland for 12 years. But then, there was talk that Spain was to invade Holland. This could spoil everything... their king was mean too!

I know, let's go to... AMERICA!

There's no king in Holland! We can worship how we like!

The cheese is pretty good too!

4

The Pilgrims' Plan

William Brewster had a bright idea... they would journey to the New World (that's what they called America). At first, the Pilgrims were afraid... America was a wild and dangerous place. There were no houses, no shops, no towns - and it belonged to the tribes that lived there with their bows and arrows. Yikes!

Finally, about 100 brave Pilgrims agreed to go. No one really knew what they would find and it would mean never seeing England again. It was a true adventure!

But there was a problem. Quite a big problem... the Pilgrims did not know how to sail! So they made a deal with some English business men: "We'll work for you for seven years if you get us to the New World" they vowed. Would you want to work for someone for seven years for free? Many of the Pilgrims didn't - in the end, only 47 Pilgrims agreed. Very soon these 47 brave and fearless souls would be onboard the Mayflower, voyaging into the unknown.

Meet the Crew

Myles Standish was a soldier. He brought guns onto the Mayflower to protect the travellers in the New World. But watch out... he was known to be very short-tempered!

Captain Christopher Jones was in charge. Before voyaging to the New World, he transported wine, wool, hats, salt, and vinegar to Norway, Greenland, France and Spain on the Mayflower. What a guy!

Francis and John Billington were well-known trouble-makers onboard the Mayflower. They were always up to mischief, getting in everyone's way. What a pair!

John Billington was the Billington boys' father. He would later cause problems when they reached the New World (go to page 22 for the gruesome facts!).

Baby Resolved was older now and Susanna was pregnant again.

In total, there were 102 passengers onboard the Mayflower, plus crew. Why were they going? Some for religion, some for adventure, some were servants, others were being paid. Some may even have been escaping the law!

Ready to go!

In September 1620, the Mayflower set sail from Plymouth they needed to start a new life in a new country.

Two ships originally set sail, the Speedwell and the Mayflower. Not long into the journey, however, disaster struck... the Speedwell was leaking! It had to be left behind... everyone got on board the Mayflower, making it more crowded than ever.

Wish list...

Unlike most ships, the Mayflower smelt nice – thanks to all the wine it had transported! Hic!

he Pilgrims and the sailors took everything

Things packed onto the Mayflower included...
- barrels of food, water and beer
- seeds and tools for planting them
- saws, hammers and axes for building houses
- cloth, knives, beads to trade with the local tribes
- guns for protection
- a fishing boat sawn into four pieces (as there was no room for it otherwise!)
- And perhaps most importantly to the Pilgrims, Bibles!

What would YOU take with you?

Onboard the Mayflower

Many of the Pilgrims got seasick... much to the amusement of the hardened sailors!

Captain Jones gave up his sleeping chamber for the sailors... what a guy!

1. A baby was born during the journey. It was named Oceanus... can you guess why?

2. The journey was long. The Pilgrims would entertain themselves by singing or reading their Bibles.

The passengers were the ship's **cargo**, so they all had to live in the dark, cold cargo decks below the crew's quarters.

3. Many people got ill onboard the Mayflower. William Butten was especially poorly.

4. Water stored for a long time would make people sick, so the main drink onboard was beer... even for the children! It didn't taste very good though.

mals onboard the Mayflower uded dogs, cats (to catch the e), chickens and even a pig n you guess what they were for?)

5. There were cannons onboard the ship in case of pirates!

6. Those mischievous Billington brothers set fire to a rope onboard... right next to barrels of gunpowder!

NO!

Storm!

A terrifying storm hit the Mayflower! "Get below deck!" the Pilgrims yelled. They were tossed from side to side. They were sick, cold and scared. Waves beat against the ship, tossing it around like a cork. Outside the storm roared. They heard the beam of the boat snap. Ice-cold water swept through the ship, ruining supplies and soaking beds and clothes. One Pilgrim even fell overboard!

The Mayflower menu

- hardtack (an incredibly hard, incredibly dry biscuit - perhaps with a stowaway bug inside!)
- salt horse (that's cow tongue soaked in lots and lots of salt)
- cheese (very, very hard cheese)

Ow! They're not kidding

Do you believe in sea monsters? In the Pilgrims' time they did! Look closely at this map from 1605. Can you see the monsters in the ocean between England and America?

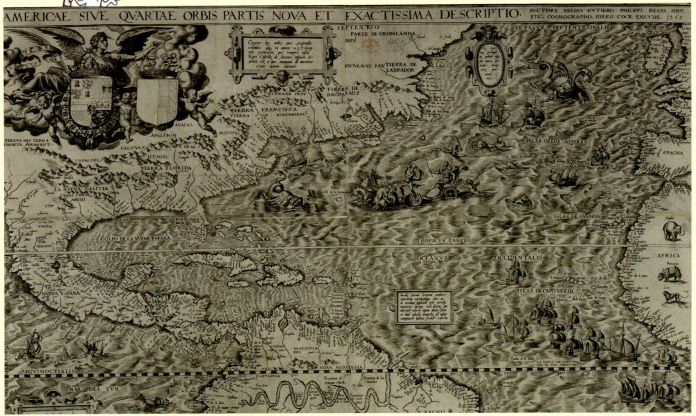

'A Modern and Quite Precise Depiction of America' by Gutiérrez, Diego (Flourished 1554-1569)

The New World

On 9th November 1620, after 66 long days and nights at sea, land was sighted. The Pilgrims rejoiced - the Mayflower had reached America!

Oo-er, they were 300 miles north off course.

- **Hudson River**
- **Cape Cod**

But there were more problems! Instead of arriving at their planned **destination**, the Mayflower had taken the sailors to a place called Cape Cod. There seemed to be nothing there but tangled woods and rocky beaches - no houses and certainly no one there to greet them. Nevertheless, the Pilgrims thanked God for bringing them safely across the ocean and set about trying to find a safe place to settle.

Unfortunately, young William Button died from his illness during the journey.

He never got to see the New World.

The Mayflower compact

When they arrived, the Mayflower passengers came up with a '**compact**', a set of rules by which to live in their new country.

Good cap, bad cap?

Although he blamed the storm, some people believe that Captain Jones tricked the Pilgrims and navigated the ship too far north on purpose. They think he did it for money.
What do YOU think?

From Ship to Shore

William Bradford, Myles Standish the soldier and some of the other men decided to take a boat to shore. They took their guns with them in case there were dangerous wild animals or even tribes ready to defend their land.

While the others explored, the Pilgrim women stayed behind and washed the clothes. It took them ages - 66 days onboard a ship meant a lot of dirty laundry!

Eww!

Cape Cod had land good for farming. It had suitable trees for building houses. Local tribesmen seemed thin on the ground too.

But there was one thing it did NOT have... fresh water! All there seemed to be was salt water - and that was no good for drinking. The Pilgrims needed somewhere else to live... quickly!

They searched and they searched, and things got worse and worse. The fishing was bad, the hunting worse and their guns were soaking wet! It was winter and getting colder by the day - many were already sick or dying.

William Bradford put his foot in an animal trap and ended up upside-down!

But who set the trap?

Mysterious findings

While they were searching for a suitable place to live, the Pilgrims found::

- woven baskets filled with corn
- a large kettle buried underground
- the remains of a house
- animal traps
- smoke billowing in the distance

What could these clues have been pointing towards?

Arrows in the woods

One morning, the Pilgrim leaders and the strongest crew members were out searching when they heard terrible cries and hollers. It was the 'war-whoop' - the sound of the **Wampanoag** tribe's war cry. Then, arrows began to fly! The Pilgrims fired their guns and most of the **tribe** ran away. Still, the arrows kept coming: one brave member of the tribe had stayed, hidden behind a tree, firing arrow after arrow at the Pilgrims.

Right or wrong?

Men from the local tribe came in the night and stole the Pilgrims' axes.

The Pilgrims found corn that belonged to the tribe and took it for themselves.

Were they right or wrong to do this? Is it ever okay to steal?

Myles Standish fired a shot and hit the tree next to him, sending splinters exploding in every direction. The man scarpered back into the woods, whooping and yelling as he went.

Friends or foes?

Everyone went back to the Mayflower to carry on the search for safety. On 16th December 1620, they arrived in Plymouth, a place discovered by Captain John Smith six years earlier. It was everything the Pilgrims needed - finally their search for a suitable home was over.

They set about building their homes - but they were cold, hungry and weak. With no fruit or vegetables to eat, twenty-two Pilgrims had got sick and died. It was a long winter.

Then one day, a tall, straight-backed man stepped out of the woods...

Meet the tribe

Samoset was the first tribesman to meet the Pilgrims. He approached them with two arrows: one headed to show war, the other unheaded to show peace. The Pilgrims chose peace and Samoset became their friend.

Squanto was introduced to the Pilgrims by Samoset. He'd had a very interesting life! When white men appeared six years earlier, they had traded beads and weapons in return for deerskins. However, one sea captain tricked him and took him captive. He took Squanto away from his family and home and back to Spain. Here, he was sold as a slave. However, he was saved by monks who taught him English. Finally, he befriended another sea captain, who brought him back to his American home. Later, he became a special friend to the Pilgrims, bringing them eels, lobster and fish to eat. He even ended up living with them!

The Pilgrims and the local tribe became friends. They got to work on a peace **treaty**, promising never to attack or steal from each other again.

The Pilgrims traded with the tribe. They had brought beads and knives with them for this and swapped them for much-needed animal furs to keep them warm.

Squanto told the Pilgrims to bury small fish. The Pilgrims must have thought this was very odd... but it worked! It fertilised the soil and made the crops grow really well!

Chief Massasoit was the leader of the Wampanoag tribe. Before the Pilgrims arrived, a disease called smallpox had killed many of his tribe. The disease had probably come from other white visitors, so Massasoit was very wary of the Pilgrims. Through Samoset and Squanto, Massasoit grew to trust the Pilgrims - especially when Edward Winslow, the Pilgrims' doctor, nursed him back to health when he was gravely ill.

20

Goodbye Mayflower

People had to stay on the Mayflower until their houses were finished. It was not a very healthy way to live! By April, there were only fifty-one people left alive. In the end, only five houses were needed.

Once all the remaining Pilgrims had houses, Captain Jones told his crew that it was time to sail back across the ocean. The captain offered to take any Pilgrims who wanted to go. In their hearts, some of them may have wanted to leave - but not one Pilgrim said yes. So, on 5th April 1621, the Pilgrims waved goodbye to their ship and their lives in England forever.

Fight for survival

The Pilgrims worked hard for the rest of the year. It was so important that they got good at farming - having enough food was the only way they would survive. There would be no school for the children in that first year - the boys and girls had to help out by shelling corn, picking mussels from the rocks or digging for clams in the mud. Some would spend the day cooking a turkey on a spit - it took all day to cook.

At least there's no school!

One day, the leader of the Pilgrims, John Carver, was taken ill. A few days later, he died. The Pilgrims needed a new leader. William Brewster was their first choice, but he said no - he would rather lead the church than the people. So the Pilgrims elected William Bradford as their new leader. He was only 31 but he was a trustworthy and upstanding kind of guy!

LEADER.

America's first murderer?

John Billington, the Billington boys' dad, often got into trouble just like his sons. When he was asked to keep watch one night, he said no - until he heard that his punishment was to have his neck and heels tied together! Nine years later, he shot a man and was hanged for his crime.

The first Thanksgiving

By the middle of October, the Pilgrims had plenty of food, more houses were finished and they were no longer in danger of becoming ill. The local tribes were their friends and they could now lead their own lives, worshipping God how they pleased. They had a lot to be thankful for and decided to celebrate.

They invited the tribespeople and around ninety joined the feast. There was turkey, wild goose, duck, lobster, eel and fish, as well as berries, vegetables and pumpkin . The local tribes killed five deer. They even helped the Pilgrim women to grind corn to make flour - this meant corn bread for everyone! And there was corn, lots of corn, even popcorn!

Together, the brave Pilgrims and lifesaving local tribes ate, sang, danced and played games. There was so much food it took three days to eat it all!

This became known as the first Thanksgiving.

Thanksgiving today

The custom of Thanksgiving still lives on. In America today, the festival is celebrated every year in November, after the Harvest.

The food the Pilgrims ate has become traditional at another time of year too... Christmas! People all over the world celebrate by eating turkey, cranberry sauce and roasted vegetables. Mmm!

24

Happily ever after?

Stories of the Pilgrims often end with Thanksgiving... but what happened after that?

 - The Pilgrims sent letters back to England saying how wonderful their new home was. Soon, more and more people sailed across the ocean to join them.

 - The Pilgrims befriended other tribes, although some were less friendly. The Narraganet tribe sent a bundle of arrows tied with a snake skin: a challenge to battle! The Pilgrims sent back a snake-skin filled with... bullets! Guess what? The tribes backed off. Wouldn't you?

The local tribes may have got on with the Pilgrims, but that does not mean that they were safe from all visitors from overseas. Other people stole from them, mistreated them and even killed them. Some got diseases from the overseas settlers. Not always a happy ending!

The Founding Fathers

The Pilgrims will forever be known as the 'Founding Fathers' of America - not bad for a bunch of misfits from Doncaster!

The people of England and America continue to have close links to this very day.   From holidays to music, from movies to restaurants, from snacks to shops, the British and American people share so much. And just as the Pilgrims mixed peacefully with the natives, both countries are now home to people from many different countries and backgrounds.

Discover Doncaster!

Doncaster, the place the Pilgrims left behind centuries ago, is still an exciting place to be. Just like the brave and **pioneering** Pilgrims, people from Doncaster have achieved so much...

- the world's most famous steam trains were built in Doncaster, like the Flying Scotsman and the world's fastest steam locomotive, Mallard!
- Doncaster is home to one of the oldest horse races in the world, the St Leger.
- many of the first aeroplanes flew from Doncaster.
- inventors like Thomas Crapper (inventor of the flush toilet), dinosaur experts, war heroes, even world-famous pop stars come from Doncaster!

What's more, you can visit Conisbrough Castle, the Dome, the Mansion House and the Yorkshire Wildlife Park, the UK's biggest walk-around wildlife centre!

The Mayflower Timeline

July 1620
The Pilgrims return to England from Holland.

1606
The Pilgrims move to Scrooby near Doncaster.

September 1620
The Mayflower sets off from England

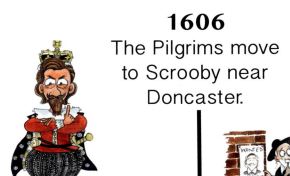

1603
King James I rules England.

1608
The Pilgrims escape to Holland.

November 1620
The Pilgrims arrive in America.

1614
Squanto kidnapped and taken to Spain as a slave.

1619
Squanto returns to America.

April
1621
The Mayflower sails back to England, leaving the Pilgrims behind.

November
1621
The Pilgrims celebrate the first Thanksgiving.

400 years later...

December
1620
The Pilgrims ttle in Plymouth.

Summer
1621
William Bradford becomes Governor.

November 2020
People from America and England celebrate 400 years since the Mayflower landed in Cape Cod. Here is the 'Illuminate' festival in Doncaster, a parade with lights, music and models to remember those brave Pilgrims who ventured across the ocean 400 years ago.

Glossary

cargo - the goods carried onboard a ship

civilisation - a way of living that is considered advanced

compact - a set of written rules

destination - the place to which someone is going

governor - someone who is in charge

Pilgrim - a person who journeys to a place for religious reasons

pioneer - a person who is the first to explore a new country or area

separatists - people who want to separate from the main religion

treaty - an agreement between two groups of people

tribe - a group of people from a particular place with a common culture and language

tyranny - when someone rules in a cruel and unreasonable way

Wampanoag - a group of five tribes living in the New World when the Pilgrims arrived

worship - to pray to God or take part in a religious ceremony

Index